Hearts' at Home

Building Solid Families in a Shaky World

Mark Finley
with Steven Mosley

Pacific Press Publishing Association
Boise, Idaho
Oshawa, Ontario, Canada

Edited by B. Russell Holt
Designed by Tim Larson
Cover photo by Juan Alvarez/Image Bank ©
Typeset in 10/12 New Century Schoolbook

All Bible texts are from the New King James Version unless otherwise credited.

Library of Congress Cataloging-in-Publication Data

Finley, Mark, 1945-
    Hearts at home: building solid families in a shaky world / Mark Finley, with Steven Mosley.
        p.   cm.
    ISBN 0-8163-1231-1
    1. Family—Religious life. 2. Family—United States. 3. Christian life—Seventh-day Adventist authors. I. Mosley, Steven R., 1952- II. Title.
BV4526.2.F56   1994
248.4—dc20   94-30539
                                                                  CIP

94 95 96 97 98 • 5 4 3 2 1

Contents

Before You Turn This Page!

Suppose you were at the end of your life. You had only one more day to live. Your mind was alert. Your thinking sharp. Your memory of the past vivid. During that last day, each major accomplishment of your life from birth to the grave passed before you in graphic detail. From the perspective of life's final moments, how would you define success? By the size of your bank account? By the number of corporate boards you sat on? By your portfolio?

Would your wife consider you a success as a husband? Would your husband consider you a success as a wife? Would your children's comments testify that you were a smashing success as a parent? There are families today who are refocusing their priorities. They are changing their schedules. They are reevaluating their communication methods. They are becoming more caring, sensitive, listening, nurturing centers of loving relationships.

Hearts at Home is not a magical key to transformed relationships. It is not some superficial cure-all for family ills. It does present practical principles that, consistently applied, can transform your relationships. The chapter "Being Married to Me" asks the question: What would our home be like if my spouse treated me the same way I treat him or her? Rather than considering the changes my spouse needs to make to please me, it evaluates what changes I need to make and how to make those positive changes. The chapter entitled "I Can't Talk to My Teenager" opens new windows on how teenagers think, why they close up so quickly, and how to get them communicating again. *Hearts at Home* is designed to be read again and again. Applying its principles can make a real difference in your home. Understanding its insights can change the most strained relationship.

The greatest power in the universe is the power of love. Love changes circumstances. Love changes families. Love restores relationships. Love defuses tension. Selfishness, on the other hand, is destructive. It ruins effective communication, destroys relationships, and tears families apart. *Hearts at Home* reveals the only source of pure, unselfish love in the universe. Tapping into God's love, receiving love from above, enables us to become channels of joy in our homes. Steven Mosley and I pray that you will personally experience an infilling of divine love as you read these pages.

Mark A. Finley

Being Married to Me

Imagine for a moment that the whole world could hear the words we unload in the privacy of our homes. What would they sound like? Imagine, for example, a husband coming home from the office in a foul mood.

Gary: "I mean, you should have known, Alice. I phoned you twice. You don't check the answering machine now?"

Alice: "It's almost ready."

Gary: "Dinner could have been ready five minutes ago. Now I have to wait. You know, I've got to start drinking milk—you're going to give me an ulcer. I just don't believe it. The bathroom towels are wrinkled. I found a slipper on the living-room floor. You didn't even hang up my bathrobe, and you know how I feel about that. You can't even clean the house. You know, you don't even work full time. I don't know what you do with all the time you've got. Jiminy! Sometimes I just don't understand—I don't understand how you don't know after all these years how to do it right. I really just don't understand you sometimes."

* * * * *

Gary has been Alice's husband for thirteen years. He's had a lot of time to think. Unfortunately, he's never asked himself one question: What's it like being married to me?

People sink into some very bad habits when they don't ask themselves the very important question: "What's it like being my spouse?" That question becomes extremely critical after a marriage has gone through many years of wear and tear. Let's look at a typical example.

Jack and Lisa had just celebrated their fifteenth wedding anniversary. It was a nice occasion—friends came over to wish them well. They had a pleasant dinner together. They talked about old times and good memories.

Then everyone said good night, and Jack and Lisa were left alone in the house, staring at each other. Two lonely people terribly aware of the wall between them; two people exhausted from the strain of pretending to be happily married.

The cracks that had always existed in their relationship now had become deep crevasses.

Jack was frequently gone on business trips. For years, their conflicts had been resolved only by his lengthy absences.

Lisa had tried to build a life of her own, getting a job and widening her circle of friends. But that wasn't enough anymore. She needed more, and she had begun to wonder if she could ever get it from her husband.

Jack tried; he sincerely wanted the marriage to work. But he wasn't very good at communicating his feelings. He tended to look for an intellectual answer to everything—reading books and pondering abstract questions—while Lisa wanted emotional support.

And Lisa, an incurable romantic, had allowed her affections to wander. She'd been crazy about Jack and almost worshiped him. But what before she had regarded as great wisdom, she now viewed as Jack's way of controlling her.

Jack tried to be more supportive. But by now Lisa

had grown quite cold. Why should he keep trying, he told himself, if his wife wasn't going to respond? And Lisa kept questioning Jack's sincerity; he was just trying to control her.

Neither of these people wanted a divorce. Their religious and personal convictions had never allowed that option. And yet they couldn't find the will to stay together. They kept groping around in the dark, bumping into each other, less and less able to trust, seeing more and more fatal flaws in each other and little hope for change.

Jack and Lisa's story hits close to home for a lot of people today. More and more marriages are falling apart after years of attempts to stay together. Marriages are breaking in the middle. Couples are giving up on ten, fifteen, or twenty years of a relationship.

Many counselors believe marriages become especially vulnerable after the kids grow up. Some partners find that raising their children was about the only thing they had in common.

Other observers talk about the strains that the midlife crisis brings on. A lot of people who've achieved success in their jobs wake up one morning, look around, and ask, "Is this all there is?"

There's another factor that contributes to marriages breaking apart in the middle. Let's be honest. In some homes, it's the women who've made the sacrifices, put up with their husbands' problems, and done what it takes to keep the family together. These women today are tired of playing that role; too often their long-suffering love turns them into victims of abuse. A lot of them are just plain tired out and upset, and they're not going to take it anymore.

All these forces pressing in on couples in midlife create one great cry from the heart: Something has got to change! I'm sure you've heard a friend or acquaintance say it: I just can't go on living this way. I'm going to snap. Perhaps that's your own secret cry: I can't take it anymore; something's got to change!

For couples under pressure, the obvious answer seems to be: Change your marriage partner. He or she is the one causing all the problems. What you've got to do is change the person staring back at you across the breakfast table.

Let's face it. Sometimes there are victims who do need to be rescued. Sometimes there are abusers who need to be directly and openly confronted. Anyone with a pattern of verbal or physical abuse who refuses to seek help is destroying their marriage.

Unfortunately, the language of abuse is now applied to all kinds of situations. Criticizing or nagging can be viewed as verbal assault. Some begin to see manipulation or an attempt to control behind every request or comment. Some people can find passive-aggressive behavior in every silence, every gesture.

Common faults can be blown up into great crimes with the language of abuse. There definitely *are* people who compulsively try to control their spouses, always putting them down, always trying to restrict their friends and interests. But the vast majority of troubled couples are caught in a web of trying to control each other in big and little ways. The road to marital pain and suffering is a two-way street.

That's why I'd like to suggest an alternative to simply changing a spouse. It's true; something's got to change! But it's not the marriage that's somehow to blame. It's the people in it. People need to change *themselves*, not just their partners.

Hoping that the next person down the line will make you happy is to hope against hope. You'll still be carrying the same baggage into the next relationship. You'll still have your same habits, your same compulsions, your same tendencies. You'll still have the same unresolved hurts.

It's people who need to change.

Listen to what counselors who've talked to hundreds of people on their second go-around say. They tell us that the most typical comment from people who are experiencing second-marriage difficulties is this: "If I'd known then what I know now, I would have worked harder, much harder, to keep my first marriage going."

When your marriage is under pressure, you're apt to see everything that's wrong, everything that's a problem—except your own behavior.

A New York therapist who'd worked with fractured relationships decided to use a novel technique. He began videotaping the sessions each couple had with him and then giving them an instant replay. The results were remarkable. Husbands and wives saw themselves on the screen exactly as they were—body language, intonation, gestures, and all. The tapes were so revealing that many couples began to resolve their disputes almost immediately. For the first time in their lives, they got an answer to the question few of us ask: What's it like being married to me?

What *is* it like? People need to change themselves, not just their marriage partners. Any relationship can be salvaged if both husband and wife are willing to let God help them change.

Now admittedly, it's one thing to talk about change and quite another thing to actually do it. After you've spent years in unhealthy ruts, it may seem impossible to get out of them. And you may well believe that the person across the breakfast table won't ever really change.

But listen again to this familiar promise from the Old Testament, and try to apply it to your own marriage. It gives hope for troubled and hardened hearts in any marriage relationship: " 'I will give you a new heart and put a new spirit within you; I will take the heart of stone out of your flesh and give you a heart of flesh' " (Ezekiel 36:26).

A heart of flesh. Yes, damaged marriages can make us hardhearted; they can set our worst qualities in stone. But that's what God's grace is for; that's what the promise of a new heart is for.

The New Testament fairly bursts with the theme of radical change. And, friends, it doesn't just apply to drunkards in the gutter or to profane atheists. It applies to our marriages as well.

Listen to Colossians 1:10, 11. Paul's prayer is "that you may have a walk worthy of the Lord, fully pleasing Him, being fruitful in every good work and increasing in the knowledge of God; strengthened with all might, according to His glorious power, for all patience and longsuffering with joy."

Yes, God gives us the power to change, the power to move out of our ruts. Let me give you a few encouraging examples of how this happens. Here are positive ways that couples can deal with what appear to be incompatible traits.

Bill is a quiet, reserved emergency-room physician who likes to ski and scuba-dive. Linda is a counselor who's very open and demonstrative about her feelings. Bill likes to take physical risks in the great out-of-doors. Linda takes emotional risks, always saying just what she feels and hoping Bill will understand.

This couple was going in opposite directions—fast. The more Linda expressed her feelings, the more Bill withdrew. The more Bill withdrew, the more Linda wanted to slam pots and pans.

Finally, the two went to counseling and discovered a wonderful concept—the way to help their relationship was to help each other. They could learn and grow from their differences. Bill came to see that it was OK to express his emotions with those he trusted. He opened up more. And Linda learned to think before she spoke. Eventually, she learned to enjoy some of Bill's favorite outdoor activities.

A reserved person and an expressive person can either push each other farther and farther apart, or they can learn from each other.

Marjorie and Steve experienced constant friction in their marriage because of incompatible traits. She was very outgoing; he was painfully shy. Usually that meant that Marjorie would beg Steve to attend some party; he'd make up some excuse; and she'd have to go by herself—alone and furious.

But instead of just changing partners, they tried changing themselves. Steve started attending a few parties. Slowly, he grew more sociable. Marjorie learned there were some activities she could enjoy quietly at home. Instead of becoming more and more extreme in their traits, these two people became more whole and healthy as human beings. They learned from each other.

Here's wonderful advice from the apostle James on how couples can become more teachable. "Let everyone be quick to listen, slow to speak, slow to anger" (James 1:19, NRSV).

That's it in a nutshell. Quick to listen, slow to speak, slow to become angry. That makes us teachable. Instead of just changing our spouse, we need to see if we can learn from our partner. What we see as an incompatible trait in the other person may be trying to tell us something important about ourselves.

Now, sometimes, it's not just a question of different traits or different interests. Sometimes marriages deteriorate because of real behavior problems. Take Lionel, for example. He was something of a malcontent who found fault with everyone and everything—most often with his wife Jean. For fifteen years, Jean tried her best, her very best, to cater to Lionel's every whim. She tried so hard to make him happy.

Well, Jean finally burned out and went for counseling. But she learned something very important there. No one can *make* another person happy. She was not responsible for her husband's happiness; he was.

When Jean accepted this fact, she became more relaxed and outgoing. The pressure was off. And Lionel woke up himself when he realized Jean no longer accepted the blame for everything. He began to occupy his time more productively.

Sometimes we need to detach ourselves from the problem behavior of the other person. We can become enablers, helping them to continue in their bad habits. When Jean decided to stop doing that, she found leverage—a positive force to lift her husband. She found that behaving in a healthy way herself nudged her husband toward healthier behavior.

Donna and Ray had for some time been caught in a pattern known as the nag-and-withdraw syndrome. Donna would nag Ray about not putting his things away and not helping her around the house enough. Ray would become silent and withdrawn. That would drive his wife up the wall, and she'd nag more.

After they went for help, Ray recognized that what Donna wanted more than anything else was physical attention from him. Her nagging was really an effort to spark some show of emotion.

Ray realized that he had leverage. By showing a little

more spontaneous affection, he could short-circuit the nagging problem. Ray and Donna began meeting each other's needs instead of driving each other up the wall.

The writer of Hebrews gives some advice that I think is especially fitting for couples wrestling with problem behavior. "Exhort one another daily . . . lest any of you be hardened through the deceitfulness of sin" (Hebrews 3:13). This verse pictures the two directions a relationship can go. You can either encourage each other or harden each other. Those problem behaviors, those deceitful sins will harden and alienate marriage partners unless you find some leverage, a positive way to encourage. And often that's by displaying healthy behavior yourself.

Later in the book of Hebrews, the writer urges: "Let us consider one another in order to stir up love and good works" (Hebrews 10:24).

If you're just reacting to your spouse's problem behavior, the marriage will harden. But if you concentrate on your own positive behavior, chances are your spouse will be moved toward "love and good works."

Recently, *Psychology Today* reported on a study of three hundred couples who'd stayed together for many years. They were asked to talk about why they had enduring, happy marriages. Can you guess what the most frequently named reason was? It was simply this: they *liked* their spouse as a person; they viewed their partner as their best friend.

Now, to couples whose relationship has deteriorated over the years, this basic attitude may seem impossible. They think they've seen too much; they remember all the ways their spouse has hurt them.

But stop for a moment. All of us at one point liked our spouse as a person. When we chose to marry him or her, we saw things that attracted us; we saw things to love. Our bride or groom had weaknesses and faults. But we didn't look at those. In the enthusiasm of our first love, we noticed only the good things.

Well, we may not be able to capture that initial infatuation. But we can recapture that initial perspective. We can make a conscious choice to look at our partner's good qualities. Remember, no matter what our circumstances, we always have a choice.We can either focus on the things we don't like, or we can focus on the things we do like. What we look at can make an enormous difference.

A young wife named Sandra walked into her pastor's office one day and poured out a long and painful story. She just couldn't do anything to please her husband Joe. Each day she dreaded the moment he'd come home from work. Joe seemed to treat her with contempt.

As it happened, Sandra was an attractive, bright woman. But her sense of rejection had turned her into a depressed, tense, and frigid wife.

The pastor decided to meet with Sandra's husband. Joe was absolutely amazed when he heard that he was contributing to his wife's depression. Like most men, he didn't understand how well his wife could read his attitude.

Fortunately, the pastor had a specific suggestion. "Joe," he said, "I'd like you to select ten positive qualities in your wife, and thank God for them. Thank God twice a day, in the morning and on the way home from work."

That didn't seem terribly difficult. And since his marriage was deteriorating, Joe agreed. He began thanking God for the things he liked about Sandra. He began focusing on what attracted him, instead of what bothered him.

Before long, Sandra started changing before his eyes.

She became more cheerful and affectionate. Joe continued to be thankful, and Sandra grew in self-respect and motivation. She broke out of the walls of her depression.

After a while the pastor asked Joe if he'd memorized his list of ten positive qualities. The husband beamed. "I'm finding new things to be grateful for every day."

A little gratitude goes a long, long way, believe me, friend. Focusing on positive qualities makes them expand. So please, don't just exchange your partner for someone else if your present mate seems unsatisfactory. Most people just end up with someone with a slightly different mix of bad and good qualities.

Instead, change your perspective. Change what you focus on. This is most effective, of course, if both partners promise to do that together. Two people looking for the best in each other can overcome almost any obstacle.

Psychologist Carl Rogers once wrote this: "When I walk on the beach to watch the sunset I do not call out, 'A little more orange over to the right, please,' or, 'Would you mind giving us less purple in the back?' No, I enjoy the always-different sunsets as they are. We do well to do the same with people we love."

Today, we're experiencing an epidemic of the wrong kind of change, people changing their partners, when what really needs to change is the human heart.

So please remember to ask that all-important question: "What's it like being married to me?"

Please remember that God can take out our hearts of stone and replace them with hearts of flesh. With God's resources at your disposal, no situation is hopeless. So start learning from your partner's differences, instead of just criticizing them.

Start using the right kind of leverage to change problem behaviors.

And start focusing on the positive qualities in your mate that once held your devoted attention.

Please don't just look for a new face as the magic solution to your problems. There are people who go through their whole lives, moving from one relationship to another, thinking happiness is just around the corner, and never, never dealing with the real problems in their own hearts, never facing what really needs to change. Don't fall into that trap.

By God's grace we can all change. We can change ourselves, instead of just trying to change our partners.

A Hole in the Family

Like a lot of little girls, Melanie secretly believed that one day her daddy would marry her, maybe when she was twenty-five.

But on one terrible Saturday she would never forget, right after Daddy had come home from a trip, he and Mommy said they had an announcement to make. They stood in front of the piano, looking very serious. Daddy had presents from his trip. And then he said he and Mommy were getting divorced. This was something that happened on TV and in the movies. Now it had come to their house. Some time after that, Melanie sat under the dining-room table, pondering that ominous word, *divorce*.

Then, when she went into her parents' bedroom, Daddy's things had disappeared. There were only Mommy's things now—hairbrushes, makeup, bottles of perfume. Melanie wondered why he'd been in such a hurry to leave.

She walked over to a cupboard at the end of the room and searched every shelf. Daddy had kept his things there. They were empty. There was only the smell of sandalwood—and a single pair of socks left behind. The little girl picked them up and held them against her cheek.

The weeks passed; winter came. And Daddy didn't

come back. Life went on for the little girl, but it didn't seem quite real. Slowly, it began to dawn on her that Daddy must have some other life somewhere, some life that had nothing to do with the little girl who sometimes hid under the dining-room table.

Melanie's story, of course, is far from unique. Countless children like her have to adjust to the reality of an absent parent. But that adjustment is more difficult than we've assumed in the past. When fathers drop out of the family, it creates a hole that only becomes bigger as the decades pass. There's nothing quite as irreplaceable as an absent dad.

In the United States, one in five children lives in a fatherless home. Of single-parent families, about 90 percent are headed by women.

A recent census in France revealed that 1.7 million children are growing up without fathers. Eighty-five percent of single parents in that country are women.

But these statistics relate only to physical absence. What's sometimes even more damaging is emotional absence. Many fathers have a hard time "being there" for their kids as a supporter and encourager, as well as provider.

Boys trying to grow up to be men without a healthy father figure face tremendous obstacles. Canadian counselor Guy Corneau summarized the emotional damage he has witnessed in the four-word title of his book: *Absent Fathers, Lost Sons*.

For a long time, men have assumed that nurture and care are the mothers' department. Mothers are supposed to bring up the kids under the roof that Dad provides. But those attitudes cheat our children of an invaluable source of support. Several studies have demonstrated that warmth and attention from Dad produce confident, skillful boys and mature, independent girls.

When Dad's gone, either physically or emotionally, there's a hole in the family that nothing else can fill, nothing else replace.

There is little that would have a greater impact on human life today than the return of fathers, physically and emotionally, to the home. Nothing would change the world more dramatically than filling that hole in the family. No revolution, no political reform, no government program—nothing would make as great a difference.

Aimless adolescents drifting into drugs or crime could use a father at home. Teenage girls about to give in to the sexual pressure all around them could use a father at home. Yes, what a difference a caring, strong father could make!

But that's where we run into our big challenge. Many men didn't learn much about caring or supporting or being a source of moral strength from their fathers. Distant fathers create distant sons and daughters.

I was very, very fortunate to have a wonderful Christian man for a father. But what about the many people who didn't? How can they learn to truly fill that hole in the family? How can they fill that irreplaceable role?

Let me tell you about one father figure who is available to all of us, no matter what our family background. There's one Father who can become a model for those who didn't have a father growing up, and He's someone who can become very real for us.

Perhaps you've guessed that I'm talking about our Father in heaven. You've heard that expression before. Maybe you're thinking He hasn't done much in your life. Maybe you're thinking He's pretty distant Himself.

Well, I'd like to explain just what this Father went through to get close to us—and what He did to break through the typical male limitations.

First of all, let's try to picture the kind of father we would want as a model. We don't just want to complain about the problem; we want to focus on the solution. We want to see if our heavenly Father can be a practical solution. What's the opposite of a distant father?

Those who have studied the matter of what kids need most in a dad have come up with four qualities.

Time. First, kids need a father who invests time with his family. Most men are driven to commit quite a bit of time to making a success of their careers. It's hard for them to see time spent just being with the kids as a valuable investment.

Clinical psychologist Ray Guarendi studied the long-term experience of one hundred successful American families. Listen to what he wrote about fathers: "What kids most remember about their father is his simple *presence.* Some of the most important memories kids latch on to about their dads evolve from routine moments in family life."

Spending time with the kids. It's a priceless investment. Nothing can take its place. Nothing we buy, nothing we work for, not even anything we say can take the place of time spent together.

I have an incredibly busy schedule; it's overwhelming on occasion. But you know, I'm so thankful that I manage to spend time with the kids, just doing simple things they like—riding bikes with Mark or playing table games with Rebecca and Debbie.

Sometimes we've been able to include them in our evangelistic work. I've invested my life as an evangelist in a lot of people around the world. But there's no investment I value more than those special times I have had with my kids.

So let's ask ourselves, How does our heavenly Father measure up in this area? Well, think about this. The

God of the Bible wasn't content to just remain the Great Provider in the sky, sending down sunshine and rain, making the earth fruitful. He wasn't content to rule from a distance. God determined to come down and invest time with us.

Listen to how the apostle John described the incarnation: "The Word [Jesus Christ] became flesh and dwelt among us, and we beheld His glory, the glory as of the only begotten of the Father, full of grace and truth" (John 1:14).

God decided that the best way to be our heavenly Father was to come down and walk on dusty Galilean trails, sail with fishermen on Lake Galilee, and mingle with the Judean shepherds.

What was God's great plan to show Himself to the world? It was simply this: to pour His life into twelve men, twelve disciples. To spend time with them—almost every waking hour, as a matter of fact. They saw how He lived every day, every moment. And as a result they came to understand what their heavenly Father was really like.

Do you have trouble investing time with your family? Jesus Christ, God-in-the-flesh, is your model. Even if you had an earthly father who invested little quality time with you, remember, God has invested everything in you. He's here, through His Spirit. He's committed Himself to be by your side. And he can make you into the parent you want to be.

Limits. The second thing kids need most in a dad is someone who will set limits. Limits create security for children. Someone described it this way: Imagine a child sitting on a chair in the middle of a dark, unfamiliar room. He will find his way around very hesitantly at first. But as soon as he knows where the walls are, the limits of the space, then he will explore the room eagerly, full of curiosity and without fear.

Setting limits involves discipline, not just punishment. As James Dobson says, "Punishment is something you do *to* a child; discipline is something you do *for* a child. In other words, discipline is aimed at teaching the child something, correcting the child."

Kids won't respect someone who merely reacts to situations, venting his or her anger. But they will respect someone who is firm in setting limits, someone who tries to correct and guide them.

Many fathers run into problems in this area because they haven't been disciplined very well themselves. When little Johnnie messes up, you just blow your top—isn't that the way it's always been?

No, there's another model of fatherhood we can work from. And that model again is Jesus Christ, especially in His relationship with His disciples. It wasn't easy trying to train those twelve men. Peter was bullheaded, always getting his foot in his mouth. Two brothers, James and John, had such bad tempers they were called the "sons of thunder." Thomas was slow to believe, and Philip was slow, period.

It was quite a challenge to train these men. But Jesus invested His life in that challenge. He corrected their narrow picture of God by having them look at a shepherd with his sheep and a father with his prodigal son. He showed them what faith is all about and what it can do. He expressed disappointment when they backed away from the truth—and great joy when they began to practice it.

In short, Jesus disciplined His disciples. He had a clear goal in mind. Through all the ups and downs of their experiences, He kept guiding them, firmly and gently, toward the kingdom. And this experience created a tremendous bond between them.

On one occasion, a crowd of people rejected Christ's teachings and were going away from Him. Jesus asked the twelve, "Do you also want to go away?"

This is what Peter answered: " 'Lord, to whom shall we go? You have the words of eternal life' " (see John 6:60-68).

There was nowhere else to go. Christ's patient teaching and correction had created a spiritual home for these men, a place where they belonged. Nothing could take that away from them.

Friend, that's the kind of father I want to be. That's the kind of father everyone can know. Because God has come here. He wants to invest His life in each of us. We need to be discipled by Christ first, before we can successfully discipline our children.

Love. What do kids need most in a dad? One final thing, perhaps the most important. They need a father who not only loves but who *shows* his love, a dad who *demonstrates* it.

A family counselor recently reported that one thing he hears most is children saying, "I wish Dad would tell me or show me he really loves me." Time after time, pastors, psychologists, and counselors hear variations on this theme—a longing for affection that is expressed.

Many men simply excuse themselves from this whole area. They say, "Well, I'm just not very good at showing my feelings outwardly. I provide for my family; I take care of things; that's how I demonstrate my love."

But that excuse doesn't help our children. It doesn't fill that hole in the family. Love unexpressed is almost a contradiction in terms. If it isn't expressed, I'm not sure it exists in any meaningful sense. If we don't show love, then love withers away.

You know our heavenly Father showed His great love in the most dramatic way possible. Think, for a moment, about Christ spreading out His arms on a hill called Golgotha. Jesus has been impaled on a cross; He's paying the ultimate penalty. His limbs are spiked to the wood.

But that's not the only reason His arms are spread wide. There is a deliberateness to everything that happens to this condemned Man; every word, every gesture is carefully measured. Christ on the cross is making a passionate statement about God's love for humankind, a statement about His eagerness to welcome us into His arms.

He calls out, "Father, forgive them." He gives the assurance, "You will be with Me in paradise." He endures the worst that humans and Satan can dish out until "it is finished." All to demonstrate His incredible love. All to draw us to Himself.

Listen to how Paul views this great event: "God demonstrates His own love toward us, in that while we were still sinners, Christ died for us" (Romans 5:8).

God demonstrates His love. He shows it graphically— a spectacle that a great crowd looks upon outside the gates of Jerusalem. He is vulnerable, exposed, torn, and bleeding, inside and out. God doesn't hold anything back, friend. He has shown us His love in a way we can never forget.

This is the God who wants to love through us. This is the heavenly Father who wants to parent through us. Whatever our emotional inadequacies, His love is big enough for the job.

Yes, a heavenly Father can help us fill that hole in our families. He can help us fill our irreplaceable role. He shows us what it really means to be present as a father, what it means to invest our time, invest discipline, and demonstrate our love. He can turn absent fathers into nurturing fathers.

Harold Hughes had never been there much for his two young girls. He had the usual reasons. His trucking business ate up almost all his time. On those evenings when he wasn't on the road, he was often out entertaining business associates.

But there was one problem, in particular, that kept Harold absent, physically and emotionally, from his family: his drinking problem. He was an alcoholic. When his wife Eva tried to talk to him about it, he would blow up. Sometimes his girls hid in the closet when he came home. When sober, Harold noticed dark circles under his wife's eyes.

Finally, Eva and the children left the house. This shocked him into making a solemn promise. He swore, before a judge, that he wouldn't touch liquor for a year. His family returned.

A few weeks later, Harold traveled to a truckers' meeting in Iowa. One morning he woke up in a Des Moines hotel—and noticed vomit in the bathroom. He didn't even remember his night of drinking. But one more promise had gone down the drain.

Things kept getting worse after that. He was putting his family through hell, and he knew it. So Harold decided to end it all one night in a bathtub with a twelve-gauge shotgun. Before he pulled the trigger, however, he thought he'd best explain to God why he was doing this.

That prayer proved to be the turning point of his life. He confessed himself a failure, a hopeless drunk, and asked for forgiveness. Harold felt that Christ came into his life that night. God the Father was very present, driving out the emptiness and self-hatred, filling him with joy. And this man submitted himself to the discipline, to the discipleship of Christ. He learned what it means to be a father by spending time with the Master.

One evening, shortly after his conversion, Harold was studying the Bible alone in his living room. He felt a nudge at his elbow and looked up. There were his two small daughters, standing quietly in their nightgowns. He stared at them for a moment; they had changed so much, and he had missed so much.

Then Carol, the younger, said, "Daddy, we've come to kiss you good night."

The father's eyes blurred. It had been so long since the children had come for his embrace. Now their beautiful, clear eyes held no fear. Daddy had come home at last.

Harold Hughes would go on to become a distinguished United States senator and governor of Iowa. He would receive many public honors. But most important to him was that moment when he realized he'd finally filled the hole in his family; he'd finally fulfilled his irreplaceable role.

His daughters wouldn't have to grow up like little Melanie—always wondering why Daddy had left for another life that had nothing to do with her. They would cherish a father who was truly present, truly there for them.

Have you been absent as a father? Is there a hole in your family? I challenge you today to consider your one irreplaceable role. I ask you to think about your most important career.

Maybe you feel quite inadequate as a father. Maybe your background hasn't prepared you very well to be a supporter, a nurturer. But will you make a commitment with me today? Will you determine to allow Jesus Christ to turn you into the parent you were meant to be? Will you invest time in a relationship with Jesus Christ so that you can invest quality time with your children?

Listen to the Children

Have you noticed something about life lately? The volume seems to have been turned up very high. There's a lot more screaming than talking, a lot more banging than knocking. Wouldn't it be great if, just for once, the whole world could turn the volume down and listen to a few small voices?

Bob Greene had seen a lot of the world in his work as a journalist. He'd learned a great deal writing a column for the *Chicago Tribune*. And he'd interviewed many interesting people as a special TV correspondent.

But Bob wasn't prepared for how much he would learn just by looking into the eyes of his baby daughter. A new world opened up for him, a world that he tried his best to record in a journal of his child's first year.

Shortly after Amanda Sue's birth, Bob wrote this: "I am of a generation that has made self-indulgence a kind of secular religion. I looked down at that baby, and suddenly I felt that a whole part of my life had just ended, been cut off, and I was beginning something for which I had no preparation."

Bob Greene knew that he would have to teach his little girl many things as she grew up. But fortunately, first, he started out by learning from his daughter. Amanda Sue had a lot to tell him, even before she uttered her first words.

Bob learned about sharing when Amanda first started holding her milk bottle all by herself. As he bent over her crib, the baby took the bottle from her mouth and offered it to him. Bob laughed and handed it back. But she shoved it back toward his mouth. It was clear, Baby wanted to let Daddy have some of that good stuff too.

Bob learned about beauty one very gray afternoon when the sun suddenly broke through the clouds. His wife picked up the baby and said, "Look, Amanda! The sun's coming out! Look at it!"

The three of them stood at the window and looked out on the street below flooded with light. Bob realized that before Amanda, he'd hardly paid any attention to the sun or the clouds.

Most of all, Bob learned what it's like to be connected, heart and soul, to another human being. When his wife and baby went on a short trip, he stood in his living room and marveled at his feelings.

"Eight months ago," he wrote, "she didn't exist. And now I find that, without her at home, there's a huge void in my life. I almost ache for not seeing her."

Bob Greene's journal, called *Good Morning, Merry Sunshine*, documents the wonder of parenthood in a charming way. But it also is a great example of what all of us parents need to become. We need to become students. We need to learn, before we can teach. We need to listen to little voices, before we can instruct them.

In many ways, our world has become a rather hostile place for children. No one can ignore the enormous problems of physical abuse and neglect. But kids are assaulted in other ways too. Our culture is turning into an "adults only" experience. It's no longer enough for movies to gently entertain. Producers must give us a steadily escalating diet of graphic violence and explicit sex.

The music blaring from our radios has grown hateful and hard edged—when it doesn't major in seduction. Even so-called "family sitcoms" can't resist off-color jokes and suggestive situations.

It's an "adults only" world out there. There's no room for innocence; the images must all be sensational. There's no room for quiet voices; we've got to turn up the volume to the max. I'm afraid we've lost something precious in the process.

Children have something to teach us. They have something to share with us. And unless we learn from them, we will be much poorer as human beings. That's the first challenge all of us face as parents, I believe. Are we learning from our kids, as well as trying to teach them? Are we open to what they have to give us?

The disciples of Christ were once caught up in an argument about who was the greatest in the kingdom of heaven. Jesus silenced their bickering by standing a little child in front of them. He said, "Unless you are converted and become as little children, you will by no means enter the kingdom of heaven" (Matthew 18:3).

What is the first step into God's kingdom? Becoming like little children. Clearly, there's something very important we must learn from them. Jesus saw what it was; unfortunately, our present world is drowning out those little voices.

We need children, first of all, because they teach us to have faith. There is nothing quite as heartwarming as the belief that children express spontaneously. They seem to have a connection with God that the rest of us usually struggle long and hard to attain.

Jesus understood the value of this pure, innocent faith. Once, He was busy ministering to some people when several mothers brought their children to be blessed by the Master. The disciples didn't think their

Master had time for those runny-nosed urchins. So they asked the mothers not to bother Him.

Jesus overheard His disciples and brought them up short with this remark. It's something very similar to what He'd told them before when they were arguing among themselves. " 'Let the little children come to Me, and do not forbid them; for of such is the kingdom of God. Assuredly, I say to you, whoever does not receive the kingdom of God as a little child will by no means enter it' " (Mark 10:14, 15).

To Christ's contemporaries, this was quite an astounding statement. He had been exposing the hypocrisy of the religious leaders of His day, and now He turns around and informs everyone that the first ones in the kingdom will be children and that heaven belongs to them! Furthermore, He declares that all of us must enter in the same way they do!

Spontaneous faith. Guileless affection. Unassuming trust. We need children because we need these qualities in our lives. Without the faith of children, adults grow too cautious, too indifferent, too rigid.

In order to lead our kids, we must first let them come to Jesus. Don't put any obstructions in their way. Don't misrepresent the loving Saviour. Let the children come, and then help nurture that innocent, pure faith.

There's another important reason we should listen to children before we teach them. And that is their spontaneous acts of giving. To be sure, kids can be quite selfish at times. "Mine! Mine!" is one of the first expressions human beings learn. Little tots instinctively hang on tight to whatever is being taken away from them.

But children can also be generous in ways adults rarely are. Do you remember what it was like?

If placed in the right situation, children just naturally share. They want everybody else to have fun, just as they're having fun. They have far fewer boundaries and prejudices than we older folk. Kids don't own an awful lot in this world, and it seems easier for them to give away what they have.

They might fight with a brother or sister over a cookie crumb and then turn around and want to give all their possessions to a homeless person they see on the street.

Jesus understood well the blessedness of possessing nothing. The same Master who called disciples to become like children in entering the kingdom also asked those who wanted to enter the kingdom to give up all their possessions.

Once, a rich young ruler came up to Jesus and asked how to obtain eternal life. The Master told him, " 'If you want to be perfect, go, sell what you have and give to the poor, and you will have treasure in heaven; and come, follow Me' " (Matthew 19:21).

What was Christ asking here? A childish act of radical generosity? Just go and sell all your possessions? No. Jesus asked this young man to divest himself of his riches because that's what this man needed to do in order to break the hold of materialism on his heart.

In our present world, saturated with materialism as it is, we need to nurture the quality of generosity. We need to affirm those childish acts of giving. And do you know how we do that best? By being generous with our children ourselves.

This is not just a matter of how much we spend on their birthdays, not how many toys we buy at Christmastime. No, it's how much of *ourselves* we give them. We haven't really taught giving until we give ourselves.

Comedian Billy Crystal was in Manhattan shooting a movie when his daughter Lindsay was to celebrate her eleventh birthday. So he called her in Los Angeles and apologized about his work schedule. But he promised that a package would be delivered soon. Lindsay was disappointed, but she thanked him for the coming present.

Later that same day, a most unusual package arrived at her front door: a six-foot high cardboard carton. Lindsay ripped it apart on the spot, and out stepped Dad! He'd flown from New York to Los Angeles right after phoning her.

Lindsay hugged her father for five minutes, crying, "Pinch me. Pinch me." She couldn't believe this unusual gift was real.

Billy Crystal's own father had died of a heart attack when Billy was fifteen. He says, "I've missed twenty-five birthdays with my father. I won't let that happen to my girls."

I have to do quite a bit of traveling all over the world in my work as an evangelist. Sometimes my schedule seems overwhelming. But one thing I do at the beginning of the year is to write in all the really important dates in my appointment book. Those are my children's birthdays, our wedding anniversary, and other special family events. These are special, sacred times that a father just can't miss. And I have to make them a priority.

We haven't really taught giving until we give ourselves.

One thing that keeps astounding psychologists who study traumatized families is this: children are extraordinarily resilient. They can endure neglect and abuse and still bounce back, still love, still hope.

Sarah Moskovitz wrote a remarkable book called *Love Despite Hate: Child Survivors of the Holocaust and Their Adult Lives*. In it she tells the stories of twenty-four persons she interviewed who had been liberated from

Nazi concentration camps as children. It's difficult to imagine more horrible surroundings for one's childhood.

This is what Sarah Moskovitz said: "The prediction for child survivors was that they would all grow up to be antisocial, severely damaged people. Actually, most are communally involved, strongly religious, and live their lives in a deep spiritual plane." Somehow these kids found spiritual values in the midst of the horrors of war and death.

It's certainly true that many children are scarred for life by destructive experiences in their homes. But the amazing thing is that so many kids *do* grow up and lead normal, healthy lives in spite of what they've been through. And here's one of the reasons: They have a wonderful gift called—forgetfulness.

A man we'll call Fred tells about the day he blew up at his daughter Lisa. He'd been under a lot of pressure at work and was in a bad mood that morning. The kids were late getting ready for school. Lisa, in particular, seemed to be just dragging around. She spilled her breakfast cereal. She left toothpaste all over the bathroom sink.

Finally, Fred exploded. He told Lisa what a terrible girl she was, just ruining his whole day. She was always doing this wrong, always doing that wrong. After his tirade, Fred stomped out of the house and drove to work.

Well, all during that day, Fred couldn't get Lisa's face out of his mind—her stunned, sad face listening to him yell. Her angry, bitter face turning away from him. He began to dread going home. He was going to have to face a very upset and indignant young lady.

Fred pulled into his driveway reluctantly, and who should run out of the house to greet him but Lisa, beaming from ear to ear. She gave Daddy a big hug, happy to see him home. The ugly incident that morning seemed completely forgotten; she was content just to be Daddy's little girl again.

Children seem to forget wrongs done to them so quickly. It's a special kind of grace they have. They don't dwell in the past, mulling over and over some hurt or disappointment. They're always ready for the joy of the present.

We need the forgetfulness of children. We need their open-armed excitement about each new day. If we keep reminding kids of the things they've done wrong, we will eventually damage that gift of forgetfulness. And we'll eventually distort their picture of God.

The words of the apostle John are words that every parent needs to hear: "I write to you, little children, because your sins are forgiven you for His name's sake" (1 John 2:12).

Forgiven, forgotten. The slate wiped clean. Transgressions thrown into the bottom of the sea. As parents, we need to discipline wisely; we need to set boundaries and correct consistently. But after we've disciplined, we need to forgive and allow the child to put the mistake behind him or her.

Yes, it's important to learn, before we teach. We need those small voices in our lives, in our world. They show us how to give up grudges. After all, God throws our transgressions into the depths of the sea. They show us how to be generous; after all, our heavenly Father has infinite riches. And they teach us about a purer kind of faith; after all, who wouldn't trust a man like Jesus?

We all need to listen to the voices of children as we step into the kingdom. As parents, we especially need to be sensitive to those voices as we guide them into the kingdom.

And you know, growing as a child of God ourselves is

the best way to become a healthy parent. We need to realize that we have a wonderful parent in heaven, a parent whose unconditional love never fails. No matter what our own childhood experience has been like, no matter how estranged we may feel from our family of origin, we can be remade in the image of our heavenly Father. He can give us grace, dignity, and self-worth.

So please, don't just stop with listening to the children. Become a child as well, a child who can rest in God's everlasting arms, who can be secure in His gracious forgiveness. That's the faith we need.

Thank God for the faith of children. Thank God for what they can teach us. Let's all resolve to learn well, before we teach.

I Can't Talk to My Teenager

Mom: Where on earth have you been?
Cindy: Out.
Mom: You didn't go out with that greasy what's-his-name, Freddy, again, did you?
Cindy: Mom! You wouldn't understand.
Mom: What do you mean, I wouldn't understand? I'm your mother. I have a right to know where you've been and what you've been doing!
Cindy: I just need a little space right now, Mom. Do you mind?
Mom: Nothing I say to you gets through anymore.

* * * *

Raising kids has never been easy. We must all face that dreaded rite of passage, the teenage years, and today, the challenges often seem overwhelming.

Teenagers are able to reason, but they're not yet reasonable.

They don't really know what they want, but they're dead sure about what they *don't* want.

Adolescents are trying to find their own identity at a time when insecurities and peer pressures are intense. And many of them begin that search by reacting against most of the things their parents stand for. Conflicts between parents and teenagers often end up in an angry cease-fire. People keep talking past each other and then finally give up talking altogether.

Some frazzled moms and dads fear they've lost control, that they can't get through—and that it's happening at the most critical time of their child's life.

Is there a way we can still keep communicating through the twists and turns of the teenage years? I believe there is. In fact, I believe that keeping the lines open is a matter of practicing a few simple principles.

Now, I'm not offering any magic answers. The most important principles are simple, but that doesn't mean they're easy. They require consistent practice. And that's exactly what I want to give you.

In this chapter, I'm going to show you the kind of communication that works. I hope that through what you read, you can begin putting these ideas into practice in your own family.

Listen first; correct later. That's the first communication idea. A lot of us think we're listening to our teenagers when we're really only hearing all the worries that keep running through our own heads. Good listening is the essential first step that leads to good communication.

Let's check out a way that parents often fail to listen. We'll look in on Cindy and her mother, the morning after.

* * * *

Cindy: Oh, what a night! I don't think I'll ever go out . . .

Mom: Honey, I told you that Freddy character was no good.

Cindy: Mom! It wasn't Freddy; the car broke down at

the club.

Mom: I just worry so much about that place—the people who go there.

Cindy: The car broke down; we had to have it towed.

Mom: That Freddy takes you to the strangest places—and the clothes you wear!

Cindy: Hello?

Mom: Oh, the car. Well, were you driving safely?

Cindy: Mom! It broke down; we weren't in an accident!

Mom: So many young kids are hit by drunk drivers these days . . .

Cindy: It was a minor thing.

Mom: There's nothing minor about accidents, dear.

* * * *

Maybe you recognize a bit of yourself in this scene. Let's face it; we parents carry around a pretty heavy load of worry most of the time. It's appropriate to be concerned for our children, of course. There are plenty of pitfalls out there for teenagers to fall into.

The problem is when our worry drowns out our ability to listen. Cindy's problem with her car didn't really register. Her mom was thinking about all the other bad things that could have happened.

Let's go back to this scene again and see what happens if Mom listens first and corrects later.

* * * *

Mom: Good morning, honey.

Cindy: Morning.

Mom: Would you like some pancakes?

Cindy: Sure. Oh, what a night! I don't think I ever want to go out in that car again!

Mom: Something happen, honey?

Cindy: Yeah, it broke down at the club. We had to get it towed to a station.

Mom: That's too bad.

Cindy: I was really worried about it at first. But it turned out it was something minor, something about the carburetor. So it shouldn't put me back too much.

Mom: Well, maybe you could save a little money if Dad checked out the engine for you. He'd probably do that if you want. But I'm glad you got it to a station.

Cindy: Oh, me too! I was afraid I was going to be stranded at that club all night.

* * * *

This time, Cindy's mom listened to her daughter more than to her own worries. And Cindy had enough space to tell the whole story.

There's a familiar appeal Jesus once made to His hearers that I believe has a special application for parents. It's Christ's appeal to help us be good listeners. " 'Take heed how you hear. For whoever has, to him more will be given; and whoever does not have, even what he seems to have will be taken from him' " (Luke 8:18).

Now, these words, of course, relate primarily to our response to the gospel, to the Word of God. But they also apply to family relationships. The principle expressed here is this: A little understanding creates more and more understanding. But a lack of understanding blocks that process, and we end up losing what little knowledge of our children we think we have. What we think we have is taken from us.

How does the healthy listening process begin? Consider carefully how you listen. That's the first step. If you find you can't communicate with your teenager, stop, and listen.

But let's move to the next step. After we listen, then

we ask. A lot depends on the kinds of questions we ask and the way we ask them. Parents of teenagers usually ask plenty of questions. But again, our fears and our disappointments often push us into asking the wrong way. Here's an example.

* * * *

Mom: Cindy, I have to ask you something. Why do you always have to make such a mess?

Cindy: I just got here; this isn't my stuff.

Mom: And why do you always have to talk back every time I open my mouth?

Cindy: I was just trying to explain to you why this was all here.

Mom: Look at it! Look! You have soft drinks on the couch, shoes, food—and what about your room? Why don't you ever clean that up?

Cindy: Mother . . .

Mom: It's too much! Just too much!

* * * *

Well, you get the picture. What trips us up as parents is that too many times, our questions are really accusations. We don't really ask; we accuse. We're arguing, unloading our frustrations.

And that awful word keeps slipping in—*always.* "Why are you always doing this?" "Why are you always doing that?" Frustration paints the worst possible picture. And we can end up nailing our kids permanently to their occasional misbehavior.

There's another principle Jesus gave His followers that speaks loud and clear to us as parents. It's very basic and simple. " 'Judge not, and you shall not be judged. Condemn not, and you shall not be condemned' " (Luke 6:37).

Familiar text, isn't it? Unfortunately, our home is the last place it's usually applied. Accusations disguised as questions judge ahead of time, condemn ahead of time. And our kids give that judging and condemning right back to us, and then some.

So, to reverse this impulse to judge, we should ask different kinds of questions. Questions such as these:

* * * *

Mom: So, how are things going with you and Freddy?
Cindy: OK, I guess.
Mom: I haven't seen him around in a while.
Cindy: Well, actually, he's starting to get pretty serious. Big time.
Mom: Big time? So you like him a lot too?
Cindy: Of course. He's one of the most popular guys in school—captain of the football team. Everybody likes him.
Mom: Well, that's nice. What do you like about him the most?
Cindy: I don't know . . . everything, I guess. I mean, he's popular, he's cute, funny, drives this incredible car. He's popular, but I've been wondering . . .
Mom: Yeah . . . ?
Cindy: Sometimes it's just hard to tell about people.
Mom: You're right, honey. Is there something that worries you about Freddy?
Cindy: Well, it's just that sometimes he puts me down in front of his friends. I mean, he's just joking, but . . .
Mom: But it makes you feel lousy, huh?
Cindy: Yeah, I mean . . . why can't he be funny some other way?
Mom: Well, you have to decide what's most important about someone who's close to you. What you value most in other people.

Cindy: You want to help me clean up this mess?
Mom: OK.

* * * *

Here, Mom's questions aren't those of a prosecuting attorney; she's a genuinely interested friend. And she helps her daughter to think more clearly about what's important and what's not. She is following Paul's advice: "Let your speech always be with grace, seasoned with salt" (Colossians 4:6).

Kids open up when we ask the right questions. It won't happen every time, but given the right moment, our non-threatening questions can start some great dialogue.

A woman once came to me and told me that she had learned to use the "banana principle" with her teenage daughter.

I wondered, "What on earth is the 'banana principle'?"

So she explained. Some time before, she'd noticed that her daughter often clammed up when they got into a discussion. The girl just wasn't sharing what was really on her heart.

So one day she got a banana from the kitchen, sat beside her daughter, and asked a question. While the girl answered, the mother, very deliberately, peeled the banana and took a bite. After she'd chewed the piece, she asked another question and took another bite. And so it went, through the evening. She found that her daughter opened up about a lot of things.

What had happened? Her mother had made sure she listened after she asked a question by chewing a piece of banana in her mouth. She didn't rush in with a comment or criticism while her daughter was answering. She just listened and chewed—and chewed and listened.

The "banana principle" simply means: Take time to listen. Ask, and then listen carefully.

Now we can move to the last important principle that

relates to communicating with our teenagers. After we've listened to them carefully and asked nonthreatening questions, we have to give some advice eventually. We have to offer guidance.

Teenagers are notorious for turning off when their parents turn on the advice machine. How do we get through? How do we make our values register?

Well, first, we can avoid one very common problem: Giving our advice in the negative. That is, always telling our teenagers what we *don't* want them to do, instead of what we *do* want them to do. You'll probably recognize this situation.

* * * *

Mom: Cindy, do you know Bobby's in his bedroom, crying?

Cindy: Do you see the mess that he made in my room! Everything's all over the floor—his trucks, his Legos. Have you ever stepped on one of those things? It really hurts! Mom, I think he even read my diary! He is always leaving a mess in my room. He's such a brat!

Mom: Cindy, I know your brother can be annoying at times, but that doesn't give you the right to put him down. You're always teasing him.

Cindy: Oh, come on, Mom; he's just a kid!

Mom: Cindy, Bobby is your brother. But you treat him like he's your worst enemy. You blow up every time he steps into your room.

Cindy: I hardly think he's got a right to complain . . .

Mom: You're on his case at the table. You bug him about his clothes. You hate picking him up at school. You don't treat any of your friends like this.

* * * *

It's usually pretty clear to us what our teenagers are

doing wrong. But focusing exclusively on that, in our advice, can end up reinforcing the misbehavior. It's infinitely better, friend, to focus on what you want your teenager to do right. That's what you need to talk about. That's what you need to give advice about.

Paul once wrote some counsel to the church in Ephesus that is still excellent advice for parents today. "Let no corrupt communication proceed out of your mouth, but what is good for necessary edification, that it may impart grace to the hearers" (Ephesians 4:29).

How do we build up our teenagers, according to their needs? How do we benefit them when they listen?

By expressing our love and acceptance, to be sure. But also by talking about what we expect of them in positive terms. Giving them a positive goal. They need to see what they should aim at, not just what they should avoid. In other words, as a parent, we need to be solution centered, not problem centered.

Let's visit Cindy and her mom again and see what could happen if Paul's advice were followed.

* * * *

Mom: Cindy, do you know Bobby's in his bedroom, crying?

Cindy: Did you see the mess that he made in my room? Everything's all over the floor—his trucks, his Legos. Have you ever stepped on one of those things? It really hurts! Mom, I think he even read my diary! He is always leaving a mess in my room. He's such a brat!

Mom: Cindy, I know Bobby can be annoying at times, but that doesn't make him your enemy.

Cindy: Oh, he's just a kid, Mom.

Mom: He's a kid with feelings, Cindy. When Bobby acts up, I want you to come to me. Just stop and come to me and tell me about it, all right?

Cindy: Mom, he doesn't deserve such nice treatment. After all, it's his fault.

Mom: Cindy, in our home we treat each other with respect. I know it's hard to be patient sometimes, but that's what we've got to try to do. You don't have to be best friends, but in this family we try to build each other up, not put each other down. So I want you to treat your brother with respect—even when you're angry. Do you understand?

Cindy: OK.

* * * *

Teenagers will not turn into angels the minute we give them positive, solution-centered advice. Nobody else changes instantly either. But if we consistently talk to our kids about the behavior we do want, that will have an effect. It will begin to register, and at some point, it will produce results.

When Dean Asher went away to a Christian boarding school, he faced a rather unusual problem—living *down* his father's reputation. It seems that Dad, Timothy Asher, had been quite a prankster in high school, and there were some teachers who remembered the elder Asher quite well. They assumed that Dean would be just another headache like his dad.

The boy was making enough adjustments as an adolescent already. Fitting in at a new school is never easy. He was a rather sensitive teenager, and the remarks of some of the teachers were really getting under his skin.

Late one night, unable to sleep, Dean called his father. As Mr. Asher listened groggily, his son spilled out all his problems. He said he wanted to leave school.

Mr. Asher said, "I'll come down there."

The boy's emotions got the better of him. "Oh, great!" he said. "You zoom down here tomorrow—Daddy's coming to save Sonny. Holding his hand."

Even as he said the words, Dean knew they weren't fair. But fortunately, his father didn't give him what he deserved. Instead, he opened up his heart. "Dean," he said, "I would do exactly the same for any friend."

And then he made a suggestion. "Why don't you slip off campus and walk to that little all-night diner down the road. I'll meet you there in about an hour. We can talk this whole thing over. And if you change your mind about leaving, you can slip back into the dorm, and nobody will be the wiser."

Later, as the two sat talking in the diner, Dean realized how lucky he was to have this man for a father. Dad listened while Dean spilled out his troubles. And then he spoke words that the boy would always remember: "We each are judged in the final count on what we do alone. If people here think you're like I was, then you can work to show them differently."

Afterward, they took a drive and watched the sun come up through the trees—neither saying a word but both enjoying the company. Dean went back to the dorm, finished the school year, and learned to be his own person.

Communicating with our teenagers can be a wonderful, life-changing thing. Yes, often they seem to shrug off our best advice. Yes, often they appear deaf to our most earnest pleas. But every parent has an opportunity during special times to make a real difference.

If we'll just listen first and ask the right questions and give positive suggestions, those special times will happen much more frequently.

By God's grace, we *can* fulfill the apostle Paul's admonition and communicate in a wholesome way that will build up our teenagers according to their needs.

Single and Whole

If you could look into the heart of a typical single mother, this is probably what you would hear:

The hardest thing is that you feel you have to do it all. Take discipline, for example. If you're a single parent, there's nobody else to play "good cop" when you have to be the "bad cop." You have to try to be the comforter right after you've had to punish. It's just hard to switch hats so fast.

Or sleeping alone with your small kids in the house—and you're supposed to be the protector, but you're scared to death, listening to every little noise.

And when you start an outside job—with small kids at home, well, you can get this super-woman complex. Got to be in control. I find that when people ask if they can do anything, I just won't ask for help. And yet inside, I'm dying for support.

Listen to another voice, that of a young widower:

I remember, shortly after my wife passed away, going to a conference with other pastors. I had recovered from the shock, I suppose, but the pain was still very intense. They were singing a chorus, and I began listening to the words, something about: "If you have the Lord, you won't need any-one else."

Well, that sort of bowled me over, and I nudged a friend next to me and said, "It just ain't so."

I hadn't given up my faith in God by any means. I believed that I still had the Lord. But I desperately needed other people too.

Today in the United States, a mother or father is missing in almost seven million households with children under the age of eighteen. There are an awful lot of mothers who have to try to do it all on their own. And an increasing number of fathers face the same challenge.

In fact, the single population in general has exploded in America, increasing over three decades from four million to nine and a half million.

Many, many people who've lost a spouse through death or divorce or who simply haven't found one yet face the challenge of being both single and whole.

In most societies, that seems like a contradiction in terms. Everything from Hollywood movies to the way churches socialize sends out one message loud and clear: You're nobody until somebody loves you; you don't fit in until somebody loves you.

And a lot of times, people try to give comfort or support in all the wrong ways. They tell you to just lean on God at a time when God seems very, very far away. Or they offer words of sympathy—and then walk away, back into their own busy lives.

It's impossible, of course, in a single chapter—or even in an entire book—to really heal the hurts of death or divorce. It's impossible to *create* wholeness for anyone else. But please allow me to give what help I can—through the voices of those who have gone through the loneliest hours and felt the deepest aches. I've attempted to condense into these few pages the best counsel people of experience have offered.

Let me start with a problem that many singles face. There is a tendency, especially in the recovery process, to go in one of two directions—either toward bitterness or toward guilt. Those are the two common dangers people face. And which direction you go depends on your personality.

Some people are more inward looking; they tend to worry a great deal about measuring up. They instinctively blame themselves if something goes wrong. These people often combine singleness with a chronic load of guilt: "If only I'd been a better wife or husband." "If only my kids didn't have to suffer the consequences." "If only I could cope better as a single parent."

Guilt is a useful tool when it points out something specific we need to correct now. But it becomes a terrible burden when it simply hauls up mistakes from the past for us to feel bad about. Guilt should never settle down as a permanent resident in your heart—that little voice always telling you you're not a real person anymore; you don't deserve to be happy.

Guilt is not a burden to be accepted; it's a problem to be solved. And the solution is God's grace and forgiveness. Yes, we've made mistakes; yes, we feel bad about the way things have turned out. But God promises us: "If we confess our sins, He is faithful and just to forgive us our sins and to cleanse us from all unrighteousness" (1 John 1:9).

Confession results in forgiveness and cleansing. So please, solve the problem of guilt; don't just carry it around, hoping it will go away.

Now, let's think of a different type of person—one who is more outward looking, one who thinks a great deal about *other* people not measuring up. These people instinctively blame someone else when things go wrong. They subconsciously assume that other people are responsible for their happiness. And they fall into bitterness as a result: "If only my ex hadn't been so insensitive." "If only my kids weren't such a handful." You get the picture.

Bitterness is a problem that needs to be solved too. If we let bitter thoughts settle down inside us, they take on a life of their own. Pretty soon, the whole world seems to be against us. How do we solve the problem of bitterness?

In Ephesians 4:31, Paul urges believers to put away "all bitterness." And in the next verse he explains how: "Be kind to one another, tenderhearted, forgiving one another, just as God in Christ also forgave you" (verse 32).

Forgiving one another, just as Christ forgave us. That's the secret. God has poured out His grace on us in Jesus Christ; let a little of that grace overflow to others. Yes, your former spouse may indeed have been insensitive, but unless you let go of that hurt, unless you forgive, you'll be stuck to that person for the rest of your life.

The two common pitfalls of guilt and bitterness really come from the same root: blame, the need to blame someone for the pain. We either blame ourselves or others. God's solution is to replace blame with forgiveness. That will free us from the past and help us get on with our lives. Please remember: Resolutions are always more important than regrets.

But even after the widowed have dealt with the shock and grief, even after the divorced have dealt with guilt or bitterness, they must face still another challenge. It is a challenge that all singles face whether they have ever had a spouse or not—the challenge of loneliness.

It hits people in different ways; but when it hits, it's often overwhelming.

Richard had just gone through a very painful divorce. His wife had walked out of his life, and he was still trying to come up with answers. Then Christmas rolled around and, as customary, he traveled to his parents' house. Richard's three brothers were there with their spouses, and everyone was having a wonderful time together. Richard's family had always been very supportive.

But then it came time to retire for the night. Richard's three brothers all went with their wives to the bedrooms in this large house. But Richard's parents took him down the hall to the small study with a narrow pull-down bed. He'd never slept there before during his many visits to Mom and Dad. *She* had always been with him.

Richard spent a very long night lying there on that narrow mattress in the study. It was finally hitting him—the loneliness, the aching emptiness, of life without that special person.

Loneliness, without a doubt, is the biggest challenge for the single individual. And I certainly don't claim that I have a pill that will cure it or a magic formula that will make it go away.

But may I offer a few suggestions for all of us, suggestions that might ease the loneliness a bit?

First, let me assure you that a lot more people care about you than you think. People at church or at work may appear rather indifferent, but many are willing to help; they just don't know how.

You may feel self-conscious as a single person. The pain may be making you withdraw from those you need. And it may be difficult to relate to happy families. But you can relate to someone. It's important to find other individuals who *do* understand, who *can* relate to what you're going through. They're out there, believe me. But you've got to reach out a little bit and find them. Listen to one woman's experience:

I never wanted much to join the church singles groups in my area; everybody seemed so intent on looking for a mate. And the support groups I went to just seemed to zero in on the problems and how everyone had been mistreated. I needed something more one on one.

Fortunately, a few other single friends started a prayer group. That really worked. Talking about the Bible and praying helped us focus on healthy things. We were building up our relationships with Christ, and that really helps your self-esteem. And we were building up each other, instead of just complaining. When I'm down and depressed, the best way to get up is to help someone else. If I focus on why, I just get worse. But you know, in that little group, each of us became something more than we would have been apart.

Different people have different needs, of course. But for many singles, finding a prayer or study group—people they can share with and pray with—will go a long way toward easing the loneliness.

You know, those of us who aren't single can help too. Even those of us looking on, who don't quite know what to do. How can we be more supportive as friends, as church members? Listen to one woman's story:

I have to thank God for sending some very special people into my life as a single parent. They didn't just say, "If there's anything we can do . . ." They just did it.

Every Sunday John and his wife would come by, pick up all my kids, and take them to their house for a pancake breakfast. Then they'd go out and play softball. It was such a gift to have that time to myself, to recharge the batteries.

It's the unexpected things that have really touched me. I remember the card I got from a church member who happened to see me at the mall. She just said that she'd seen me with my kids and loved to just watch us and thought I was doing a good job as a mother. And that she always prayed for me. Something like that makes your day; it makes your month.

All of us need to reach out in large and small ways. All of us need to be more of a family—sticking together, holding up those who stumble, embracing those who feel alone, encouraging those who are about to give up. That's what it means to love one another as Christ has loved us. That is what eases the loneliness.

But let me make one last suggestion. No one enjoys the pain of being alone. But everyone needs to understand that the pain can also be an opportunity. Perhaps not many of us covet the gift of celibacy, but we can claim, in singleness, a gift.

To put it simply, loneliness can drive us into the arms of our heavenly Father; single individuals can experience His love in a way that perhaps few others do. There's a beautiful passage in Isaiah that suggests this:

"Do not fear, for you will not . . . remember the reproach of your widowhood anymore. For your Maker is your husband, the Lord of hosts is His name. . . . For the Lord has called you like a woman forsaken and grieved in spirit, like a youthful wife when you were refused," says your God. . . . "But with great mercies I will gather you. . . . With ever-lasting kindness I will have mercy on you," says the Lord, your Redeemer (Isaiah 54:4-8).

I love that passage. It speaks of the wonderful, nurturing love of a heavenly Father who gathers up the forsaken, treats the abandoned with everlasting kindness, and calls Himself "Husband and Redeemer."

You know, God has designed every human relationship to portray something about Himself. We're all familiar with the picture of Him as heavenly Father. But God is also described as One who comforts us just as a mother comforts her children (see Isaiah 66:13). God is the Brother who has come in human flesh to dwell among us and share our troubles. And God is also the beloved Son, faithful in carrying out His Father's will.

All human relationships can teach us something about our Creator. That's what He designed them to do. That means all of us, whether single or married, can grow toward God in a variety of relationships.

But it also means something else. The Creator of all these precious relationships can bypass them if He so chooses. He can become father, mother, husband, wife, sister, or brother. He can minister to us directly.

Again, God's plan is to bless us through all our relationships. But if some priceless relationship on earth is broken, He can come in and bridge the gap. He has promised to love us as husband, as brother, as wife, as whatever we need. Our pain can be an opportunity. Our loneliness can help us know God in a way we may never have experienced otherwise.

A Moslem noblewoman once brought her grandson to a Christian hospital in Rawalpindi, Pakistan, for an ear examination. Her name was Bilquis Sheikh. Her husband had left her some years before. Bilquis was respected in her community; she had a beautiful home, plenty of servants, and plenty of money. But she could not shake a crushing sense of loneliness. She had everything in this world—except someone to ask, "How was your day?"

Well, the physician who came to the examining room was Dr. Pia Santiago, a woman of vibrant Christian faith. Dr. Santiago noticed that Bilquis was holding a Bible. Quite curious, she asked, "Madam Sheikh, what are you doing with that Book?"

As it turned out, this stately woman had been studying the Bible and the Koran for some time, earnestly searching for God. It seemed a hard quest indeed. She was intrigued by Christianity but found it somewhat confusing. Bilquis told the doctor, "You seem to make God so—I don't know—personal."

As they chatted, Dr. Santiago suggested that Bilquis might like to find out for herself why Christians felt this way about God. She said, "Why don't you pray to the God you're searching for? Talk to Him as if He were your friend."

Bilquis just smiled, a little indulgently. It was like being told to talk to the Taj Mahal.

But then the doctor leaned closer, took Bilquis's hand, and said, "Talk to Him as if He were your father." Those words shot through the Muslim woman like electricity.

In Pakistan, the idea that God was a father, that He had children, was blasphemous. How could the Great One be brought down to a human level?

But what if God really was like a father? On the way home, Bilquis couldn't get that thought out of her mind. Hours after going to bed, it kept her wide awake. She fondly recalled how her own father would put everything aside to listen to his beloved child. Suppose, just suppose, God were like that.

Finally, sometime after midnight, Bilquis got up and knelt on the rug by her bed. She was trembling with excitement and uncertainty. Looking up toward heaven, she spoke aloud, "Oh Father, my Father—Father God!"

This lonely woman was not prepared for the surge of confidence that followed. Suddenly, Bilquis didn't feel alone at all; God was present. This is how she described the experience: "He was so close that I found myself laying my head on His knees like a little girl sitting at her father's feet. For a long time, I knelt there, sobbing quietly, floating in His love. I found myself talking with Him, apologizing for not having known Him before. And again came His loving compassion, like a warm blanket settling around me."

Nothing in this woman's past had prepared her for such an encounter with a heavenly Father. From what her own religious culture had taught her about God, she could not imagine Him meeting her needs as a forsaken woman. But that's exactly what God did. He became father, husband, brother. And Bilquis went on to build a vibrant, fulfilling relationship with Jesus Christ as her Saviour.

God can do the same for each one of us. No matter how forsaken we may feel, no matter how painful our previous relationships may have been, no matter how deeply we may have sunk in loneliness, God can still minister to us personally as the nurturing mother, as the compassionate father, as the devoted husband. He can build us up in areas where we've been torn down; He can fill us when we feel aching and empty.

It's true that God has designed us to need other people. We need healthy relationships. And He frequently reveals Himself through those relationships. **But reaching out to other people best begins by our** reaching up to God. Healing begins by our getting in touch with the Great Physician.

Let's begin that process right now.